INNER MEDICINE

By James Barton

Best Wishes

From

James Barton

VirtueScience.com

Inner Medicine

By James Barton

"When you are deluded and full of doubt, even a thousand books of wisdom are not enough. When you have realized understanding, even one word is too much."

Ancient Teacher

"Teachers open the door, but you must enter by yourself."

Ancient proverb

Contents

1

Introduction

All wisdom and all virtues such as bravery, gentleness, kindness and steadfastness already exist within you in perfect form.

Vices and imbalances such as cowardice, weakness and clumsiness are caused by not accepting the various aspects of yourself.

Virtues in your everyday life can be developed by simply accepting the various aspects of yourself and allowing them back into your life.

This guide will show you how.

The simple but powerful techniques contained here will enable you to:

Be calm and relaxed in every situation

Eliminate habits and self-limiting beliefs by dealing with their root cause

Improve intelligence

Increase your capability in any field of endeavour

Increase physical and mental vitality

Understand yourself and those around you

Improve your character

+Much more than you now believe possible.

2

How to Read this Book

Firstly, it is not intended that you believe anything in this book blindly or without thought. There is no need to convince you of any doctrine whatsoever and any such effort would be counterproductive. Blind acceptance or rejection will not help you in understanding and applying the wonderful techniques contained here. As long as you are willing to think carefully about and experiment cautiously with the information in this book, I am convinced that you will come to appreciate its great value. Thus appreciating its value, you will study more deeply and practice the exercises with greater enthusiasm gaining considerably from doing so.

Secondly, as you read and apply the knowledge and exercises within this book, your awareness about the previous chapters will correspondingly increase. Therefore it is very useful that you reread previous chapters and continue to apply yourself to the earlier exercises as you progress. You will find that any parts you may have found difficult to understand will become clear in the light of the increased awareness that you have gained from later chapters. The varied exercises are designed to complement and enhance each other, so when you are familiar with the text, it is natural that you combine the various techniques as you see fit.

3

The Virtues

A virtue is a particular quality of being that is the correct and most natural way of dealing with a particular aspect of reality. Almost all religions and secret societies have their own particular list of virtues that they would have you aspire towards. Such lists can act as a useful guide and reminder of how we can best live. Unfortunately such lists are incomplete and arbitrary. The compilers of such lists and philosophies, whilst sometimes wise, must have been ignorant of the true nature of the virtues.

The various Human languages are distorted and incomplete maps of a beautiful and universal conceptual matrix. It is wonderfully symmetrical and interconnected. It is intimately related to every part of your life.

Just as a small number of letters can combine to make countless words and just as all the myriad substances in the world are formed from a comparatively few chemical elements so all the concepts and situations, in their infinite variety, are made up from a limited number of simple conceptual elements. The branch of the universal matrix that we are concerned with now is the virtue matrix. The universal matrix of virtues is the ideal blueprint for our character's development. In fact our true nature, underneath the various false beliefs and rubbish, is identical to it. All the parables and teaching stories in the world are contained within it. By its' very nature it is beyond dogma and sectarianism. It is, in short, the underlying unifying bridge which connects all spiritual and mundane schools of thought.

Virtues come in pairs which are complimentary to each other: the opposite of a virtue is always another virtue. If we internally prefer one virtue to its opposite partner, it becomes over extended and imbalanced whilst its partner becomes weak and stunted.

4

Examples of the Virtuous Opposites

BRAVERY and CAUTION are a complimentary pair. If I do not accept the CAUTION within me I will tend to be RECKLESS and take too many risks. On the other hand If I do not accept the BRAVERY within me, I will tend to be cowardly and miss out on opportunities.

Most people believe that the opposite of STRENGTH is WEAKNESS but this is not so. WEAKNESS is actually a LACK of STRENGTH. The opposite of too little force (WEAKNESS) is too much force (ROUGHNESS). The actual opposite of STRENGTH is GENTLENESS. They are a single state. Perfect STRENGTH must also be perfectly GENTLE otherwise it would fall into ROUGHNESS. Perfect GENTLENESS must also be perfectly STRONG otherwise it would fall into weakness.

The opposite of perfect HUMBLENESS is perfect MAJESTY. They are a single state. It is impossible to be ARROGANT without also being INSECURE. These concepts have to do with self-worth. REVERENCE and AUDACITY have to do with the worth of others. Lacking REVERENCE for someone we fall into rudeness. Lacking AUDACITY we fall into idolization. So HUMBLENESS, MAJESTY, REVERENCE and AUDACITY are all connected by the concept of worth. Every virtue is a member of a specific group of four virtues connected by a simple concept.

5

Exercise One: Overview

The mind attunes to that which it focuses on. Write down all the virtues you can think of. Knowledge is power. Write down all the vices you can think of. A vice is merely a lack of a particular virtue. Every virtue has an opposite virtue and so every vice has an opposite vice. Link together as many virtues with their virtuous opposites along with their corresponding vices. This can be more easily done by writing each concept onto a separate piece of card so that you can move them around as you will. Feel free to use a dictionary or thesaurus to help you.

Every virtue is associated with a particular basic concept such as danger, information or resources etc. Try and group the virtue pairs according to their nature. For example bravery and caution are connected with danger. Honesty, discretion and openness etc. are connected with information.

Is the virtue active or passive, giving out or keeping in, to do with the self or the non self? Does the positioning of the virtues in your matrix reflect these qualities?

The idea of symmetry is not an intellectual ornament. It helps us to see all the virtues as equal and thus removes the many prejudices and preferences picked up from particular past experience. Furthermore rigorous symmetry will reveal gaps in your knowledge or unnecessary repetition of the same concept under a different name. Your matrix should be perfectly complete at the same time as being perfectly simple: clarity and comprehension will be the result.

6

Summary of Exercise One: Overview

To do this exercise perfectly is to have uncovered and have a good understanding of the universal matrix. True your particular words and labels may well differ from country to country and person to person but the underlying concepts and correspondences will be found to be the same for anyone who studies them deeply.

It is unlikely however that you will attain that level of coherence on your first try. You will no doubt have a ragged and incomplete matrix with some degree of error. As you progress with the other exercises, come back again and again to this exercise to revise your work. I promise you that an inherent beauty, symmetry and completeness will emerge for you and you will not regret the effort you have spent. By calling forth your innate understanding and by focussing on the virtues, many inner prejudices and false notions will automatically fall away from you. You will then begin to embody the qualities necessary for a truly fulfilling and successful life. We will study the matrix further in a later chapter.

7

Beliefs

Whenever we reject a part of ourselves, it falls into semi-consciousness.

Beliefs can only exist in semi-consciousness. Think for a minute and you will see that it is so. If you are truly aware of something, no beliefs about it form: you just experience it directly as it is. Throughout your life beliefs and hypnotic suggestions have been collecting in the areas of semi-consciousness within you. It is probable that right now you have many negative and false beliefs about yourself and the world around you. There are thousands of self-help books that will tell you how to change your beliefs and teach you how to think positively. Most will produce positive effects in your life if you apply a little effort. Unfortunately the effects can be short lived: The root of the problem is missed. It is like chopping the tops of weeds or sculpting a hedge. In a while the weeds will grow back and the hedge will become untidy again. Nevertheless, clearing away the beliefs is a useful exercise in order to tackle the root: semi-consciousness which is caused by not accepting the various inner parts of ourselves.

8

Two attitudes towards Truth

Some people cherish their own beliefs and opinions to such an extent that they ignore direct evidence to the contrary. They are not really interested in the truth as much as they are in defending their own beliefs. Such people fear the truth and often labour under thousands of negative and crippling attitudes and beliefs their whole lives leading to needless suffering.

The other type of person is loyal to the truth- whatever it might be- over their own beliefs etc. Such a person is humble enough to realise that they don't know it all and has a natural curiosity about the world around them. If someone like this is proven wrong, they are not defensive: in fact they are delighted for it means they have moved closer to the truth.

So what type of person are you? If you can sincerely and whole heartedly perform the following exercise, then you have loyalty towards the truth whatever it might be.

Exercise Two: Letting Go of False Beliefs

Relax and silently declare to yourself that you wish to let go of all false beliefs that you hold no matter how long you have held them or how much you may have cherished them. As you do this, visualise in your mind an appropriate picture which is symbolic of the inner cleansing that you are undertaking. For example, imagine your false beliefs as a wall that is then smashed down. You could imagine your false beliefs as darkness that is being replaced by the light of direct awareness or imagine all your beliefs on paper that is then burnt to pure ashes that blow away. If you feel unable or unwilling to let go of all your beliefs, just pick an area or a particular belief and work on that.

Now, still relaxed, simply allow yourself to love Truth. Trust in it and be open to it. It is entirely beneficial and safe to do so. You can do this exercise any time silently and easily. Eventually it will no longer be necessary as you will have totally and naturally reintegrated the correct attitude into your everyday life.

Summary of Exercise Two: Letting Go of False Beliefs

This exercise will dissolve away many barriers to your understanding and natural wellbeing. Some beliefs will instantly dissipate. Others may take a little longer. Now that you have uplifted your attitude towards the truth you will be more open to logical persuasion and genuine evidence and you will be protected from those around you who would have you believing self-limiting rubbish etc. Also, because you have reduced the false propaganda against various parts of yourself, you are in a much better position to accept and reintegrate them.

11

More about the Virtues

The inner qualities of your nature naturally radiate outwards into your everyday life. If they are submerged, it is you and you alone who is submerging them. This pushing down of your inner qualities takes a continual moment to moment effort to maintain. The resulting inner tension and strain results in emotional and physical tension too. If you could simply stop the pushing down of your inner qualities, they would rise up into your everyday life of their own accord. When you lovingly reaccept a part of your nature, the semi-consciousness connected with it disappears and so all corresponding beliefs/habits collapse like a house of cards. Having re-established friendly relations with an aspect of your being, you have released an inner tension. There is then no pool of dark semi-consciousness for any further corresponding beliefs/habits to form.

12

Exercise Three: Awakening the Virtues

By their very nature the virtues within you are loveable. Simply focussing your awareness on a virtue will help natural reintegration.

Relax physically and inwardly. Choose a virtue that you want to reclaim. Let go of any false beliefs you may still be holding about it. Silently affirm that you love and accept that part of your nature and visualise it as a light flowing from within, nourishing and fulfilling every part of your being: actually imbuing every part of your being with the special quality of the virtue. Silently affirm that you are willing for yourself and your circumstances to change and be assured that the changes can only be beneficial. Now concentrate your efforts on the virtue opposite to the one you have chosen and repeat the same procedures. Allow yourself to see the two virtues as a single harmonious state. Let go of any preferences you have for one virtue over another: They are both an essential part of your being.

 Repeat the exercise a couple of times with each virtue you want to work on. Over time you should work systematically through all the virtues. A good quality matrix from Exercise One will ensure that none of the virtues are missed.

13

The Virtues Are Interconnected

Every virtue is reflected in every other virtue. To uplift one virtue is to help uplift every other virtue. To perfect one virtue is to perfect all virtues. For example, perfect bravery must also be humble, gentle, spontaneous, patient and compassionate and so on, through every other virtue, otherwise it would not be perfect.

By reintegrating bravery you are, to some extent, automatically reintegrating it into every other aspect of your being. So if your patience or compassion for example falter when danger is near, then boosting your bravery will help heal your patience and compassion. This general principle can be harnessed to a greater extent by reuniting virtues in a conscious way.

14

Exercise Four: Reuniting the Virtues

Relax inwardly and outwardly. Choose two virtues you wish to reunite (e.g. spontaneity and gentleness). Allow your spontaneity to be gentle and allow your gentleness to be spontaneous. See them as two separate qualities merging and mingling into each other, glowing with loving cooperation. Know that in reality they always have been one with you and each other. Realising this, manifest them in your everyday life. Let the qualities (in this example: spontaneous gentleness and gentle spontaneity) infuse every part of your nature.

15

Every Virtue is Useful in Awakening the Other Virtues

Every virtue is a unique power that is ever ready to help you in awakening the other virtues and in all ways maintain balance and harmony. Thus every virtue is an individual pathway to overall wholeness and well-being.

16

Examples of Individual Pathways

If you attain complete spontaneity, your every thought and action can only arise from the virtuous mind. Living continually in the present moment you bypass any beliefs or habits which you will notice are always linked to past or future: never the present reality, which can only be perceived directly.

If you attain complete bravery then all the fears and aversions which acted as barriers to the various aspects of your being will collapse.

If you attain complete compassion you naturally love and accept all the previously rejected aspects of yourself thus fully reintegrating all your inner qualities.

17

Exercise five: Unifying your Virtue Matrix

Write down and contemplate as many "individual pathways" as you can. Choose a virtue and try to consciously use its special quality to further awaken itself and all the other virtues within you. Visualise all the virtues as one light, one awareness, beyond labels and in unity with you now.

Vices: Yours

As you gain an understanding of the virtues and vices, you will begin to notice imbalances in your character that you had previously glossed over: either being unaware of them, mistakenly considering them to be positive or mistakenly seeing them as inevitable and inescapable flaws in your character. This recognition of previously unnoticed imbalances is certainly not a cause for dismay, on the contrary it is a sure sign of welcome progress towards the ideal state of perfect contentment and perfect concern. Living in such a state means you have avoided the twin imbalances of over concern (i.e. worry) and over contentment (i.e. complacency).

All your own vices are caused by a lack of love. There is nothing particularly wishy-washy or new age about this statement: it is a fundamental principle upon which this work is based. Accepting this principle deeply will protect you from any feelings of self-loathing which only serve to maintain or worsen the particular imbalance.

If you can condition yourself to feel compassionate and loving towards yourself despite any vice that you have just noticed yourself displaying, you will find that it will dissipate. Your natural virtuous nature will then resurface effortlessly.

Exercice Six: Dealing with Your Own Faults

Silently affirm to yourself that you are loveable even when in error. Forgive yourself for past sins. Allow yourself to feel new and act differently in the future. View your past faults as temporary clouds covering your innate sun of goodness. As you breathe in draw the necessary lessons and wisdom from your past. As you breathe out let the synthesis of your understanding affect your attitude and behaviour in your everyday life.

Love and accept the vice you are working to resolve as well as the vice opposite to it. Contemplate the simple truth that by loving and accepting the extremes we effortlessly embody the middle way that is a synthesis of both qualities.

Summary of Exercise Six: Dealing with Your Own Faults

In performing this exercise you have reduced the possibility of the vice reoccurring and should it reoccur its negative potency will be lessened.

Vices: Other Peoples

The outside world and other people in particular, act as mirrors to our inner state. If someone with a particular vice creates a negative reaction within you, you can be sure that you have a corresponding inner problem regarding the associated virtues. Such people act as a useful guide, showing you where to direct your efforts of reintegration. Making an effort to love those around you will have a direct effect on the corresponding parts of your own nature. Making an effort to love your inner aspects will have a corresponding effect on how you view others and so how they react to you. Now I must make it clear what I mean when I say "love other people". It does not mean that we do everything for them or always put their needs above our own. The love I am talking about is virtuous love: all the virtuous opposites are at one with it. For example: prudence as well as generosity and steadfastness as well as flexibility.

22

Exercise Seven: Accepting Others Despite Their Faults

Relax inwardly and outwardly. Allow the problem person to be new: don't hold onto any negative expectations about them. Inwardly declare that you forgive them. Visualise them surrounded by the lovely light of unconditional love. Imagine the light actually penetrating their temporary negative behaviour and outer personality: penetrating gently and beneficially to the painful and rejected parts of their personality. Actually love and accept those parts of their selves that they presently cannot. Know that in doing so you are helping your own inner qualities resurface.

23

A Deeper Understanding of the Matrix

The purpose of this chapter is to enable you to refine the virtue matrix that you constructed in Exercise One. Your matrix will then, more and more, accurately reflect your own inner mind and the conceptual universe. There is a part of your nature that is ever virtuous and ever conscious: your true nature. Your true nature already has a perfect understanding of the virtues. By deepening your everyday understanding of the virtues you naturally attune to that pristine part of your nature. This attunement is like a bridge that allows your true nature ever greater expression in your everyday life.

24

Compound Virtues

According to the principles of simplicity and completeness, every virtue in our matrix should be of the same order of complexity. The chemist acknowledges the vast variety of substances but in his periodic table he only includes the simple chemical elements.

Water is not a chemical element: it is a compound of two chemical elements. In the same way some of the concepts that you consider to be elemental virtues may actually be a compound of two or more other virtues. If you have a virtue in your matrix that you are not sure about, you should check to see whether or not its quality and meaning can be made up from a combination of other virtue elements. If so then it can be safely discarded from your matrix as its compound qualities are already present within your matrix in a purer form.

25

Gaps in the Matrix

If you know the quality of a virtue, by inferring it from its opposite quality etc. but you cannot think of the correct name for it don't worry. It may be that the language you are using has no name for it. This is the fault of the imperfect language and not the universal matrix! In any case just simply make up a label for it out of a few appropriate words, e.g. "OPPOSITE VIRTUE OF ..." .This will suffice as a handle for your inner exercises and that is the most important thing. Each virtue does have a more scientific name which describes its meaning more precisely. This will be discussed in the next chapter. There is an even more profound name for each virtue that the most discerning readers will appreciate, but that is beyond the scope of this book and the knowledge of the author!

26

Beyond the Elemental

It should be noted that although we are dealing with elemental virtues they themselves are formed from combinations of even simpler conceptual elements. By uncovering these elemental concepts and noting down their combinations you can be sure that you are on the right track. As you discovered in Exercise One, every virtue belongs to a group of four virtues. This indicates that all four share a conceptual element. The scientific name for a virtue is composed of the simple conceptual elements that make it up. For example, strength, gentleness, steadfastness and flexibility all share the conceptual element "FORCE".

Strength is the [GIVING OUT] of [FORCE] from the [SELF],

Gentleness is the [KEEPING IN] of [FORCE] from the [SELF],

Steadfastness is the [RESISTING] of [FORCE] from the [NON SELF],

Flexibility is the [ACCEPTING] of [FORCE] from the [NON SELF].

With the new knowledge you have gained from this chapter go back to Exercise One and review your work. Note: The data contained in this section should not be accepted without thought. Contemplate it and try to apply it to your studies but hold your own insights in equal regard. Test and test again the assumptions that you hold and the things that you are being told: the rubbish will fall away and the truth will hold firm.

27

The Unknown Virtue

In the future, if you study well, there will come a point when you have a complete understanding of the virtuous matrix: you will have noted and categorized every virtuous element possible. I myself, at the time of writing, have not attained such a level of understanding. I am just a student on the path. Despite the fact that there are gaps in our knowledge, i.e. virtues unknown to us, there is still a way that we can increase their qualities within us. By utilising the concept of "the unknown virtue" we have available to us a way of reintegrating aspects of our nature that we do not even have a knowledge of.

28

Exercise Eight: Reintegrating The "Unknown Virtue"

Relax inwardly and outwardly. Acknowledge to yourself that there may be some qualities within your nature that, consciously, you do not even know exist. In your minds' eye send the light of love and awareness into those mysterious parts of your nature. Let go of all the false beliefs you have about yourself and the world around you. Simply release any inner tensions that are pushing down the unknown virtues within you now. Allow yourself to feel different as you visualise the previously unknown qualities flooding out into your awareness. Inwardly feel every part of your being infused with new power. Now listen carefully to your inner dialogue, try and notice any pictures or feelings that come into your mind. These perceptions may be inspirational clues that can shed light for you on the conceptual matrix or offer other useful insights. Visualise all the virtues intermingled as one light shining in boundless harmony.

29

Utilising Semi-consciousness

The purpose of this book is to help the reader become more conscious. This increased consciousness is the real inner medicine. Revealing and alleviating the areas of semi-consciousness within you is the best approach to regaining your original wholeness. However, there are secondary and supplementary techniques which utilise the existing semi-consciousness within you to create helpful changes in your life.

By experiencing how to change our habits and beliefs we are supporting the primary goal of transcending them. Naturally the changes we make should move us towards the universal virtuous matrix. As we succeed with these secondary techniques and gain satisfaction from this, we should constantly keep in mind that the overall goal is towards consciousness: we should not be content with positive believes and habits but see them only as a stepping stone or temporary measure.

30

Mental Association

When the mind experiences two or more things together it, from then on, associates them together. When the mind is reminded of one of the things, the other is also remembered to a degree. One of the reasons why people display their medals and achievement awards etc. is because they evoke a little of the original good feelings associated with the achievement: it helps them to feel like a winner and so continue to act like a winner.

31

Exercise Nine: Positive Association

Look around your living area and try to identify any objects which make you feel bad because they remind you of negative past experiences or for any other reason. If you can remove them/replace them why not do so?

Do you have any objects that you associate with happiness and success hidden away from view? Why not display them more prominently for positive results?

32

Social and Universal Association

Apart from your own personal associations there are some things that are generally associated with particular feelings or concepts. For example cleanliness and tidiness are associated with order and efficiency etc. whilst dirty and messy areas are associated with squalor and degradation to some degree. Certain images, colours and forms can evoke beneficial feelings and mental attitudes within us.

33

Exercise Ten: Enhancing Your Surroundings

Why not optimise your living area by eliminating any negative images and increasing the positive?

34

Anchoring Positive Associations

There was once a case of a mental patient who lived at a certain residence and was making no progress at all: in fact his insanity and delusions were worsening week by week. For one reason or another he was moved to a different residence and there he began to improve slowly but surely until the point where he was almost able to lead a normal life. Unfortunately, for whatever reason, he had to move back to his former residence. Back in his old room again, his insanity returned and the good work that had been accomplished was reversed. This sad story illustrates the law of association that we are also to some extent subject to, depending on our levels of semi-consciousness. The reason that the mental patient's insanity returned was because his mind associated the room and its many features with the insane complexes that had developed in his semi-conscious mind. The visual and other reminders in the room were all it took to trigger a relapse. Have you noticed that certain places, situations and people always seem to trigger the same negative behaviour patterns within you? The next time this happens to you perform the following exercise to anchor positive associations to the external stimuli.

35

Exercise Eleven: Anchoring Positive Associations

Relax inwardly and outwardly and smile gently. Allow your eyes to rest on a particular feature of your surroundings for a second. At the same time smile confidently and repeat a positive affirmation such as "I feel happy and relaxed", "My true virtuous nature radiates through every part of me" or "I choose to let go of all false beliefs". Alternatively repeat a simple word such as "beauty", "calmness" or "determination" etc. Now allow your eyes to rest on another feature of your surroundings for a second and repeat a different positive affirmation. Repeat this procedure a few times until you feel a sense of power, calmness and wellbeing.

36

Summary of Exercise Eleven: Anchoring Positive Associations

If you perform this exercise properly, you will build up a web of positive associations with the external object. When you then encounter it normally and glance at a feature that you worked on, favourable feelings are triggered within you. More than one feature anchor is likely to be triggered in the course of an encounter, thus enhancing and supporting the beneficial effects. Note: it is not necessary to be physically there when anchoring positive associations onto an object. By picturing the object in your mind you can perform the exercise anywhere.

37

Exercise Twelve: Deepening Positive Association

This text has been specially formulated to increase your feelings of wellbeing in general and to deepen your positive association with this book in particular. The purpose of this deepening is to facilitate your study and make beneficial changes within you easier to accomplish. A light trance may be induced within you as you read. This is perfectly safe and beneficial but if you feel uncomfortable with the idea, instead of reading on, you should skip to the next chapter now. This exercise is very easy to perform: all you have to do is relax a little and read on! Right now as you read these words, as your eyes focus on the black shapes of the letters and the white spaces in between you notice your breathing and the feeling of your clothes on your body. Your body already knows how to respond to the pure life entering into you as you breathe in and to the growing peace as you breathe out. Your awareness expands to the area around you and now you focus back into the comforting text. The black shapes of the letters and the white spaces in between can carry you deeper into relaxation, gently and easily, deeper and deeper. Sleep. The words on this paper are also in your minds' eye too. They resonate there with meaning. The black shapes and the white spaces represent bliss and happiness to you now as you read these words, as you breathe slowly and easily. You notice yourself smiling as you remember the last time you really felt alive. Smiling as you relive the best time you really felt happy and relaxed. Beautiful feelings welling up inside you. These feelings will stay with you for hours, maybe even longer as you feel loving warmth emanating from every sentence. As you feel pleasant calming sensations spreading through your fingertips and hands, penetrating every part of you. Just relax as the spaces in between the words hold your attention and your healthy curiosity wonders what would happen if you read this text again. Deeper. You are turning a new page in your life, reminded of the times that you have made successful changes in the past. Very deeply relaxed. The black letters on this page, like soothing music, can heal your heart if you let them and the inner voice you use, as you read these words, wants the best for you. If you want, you can summon your inner power right now and decide to help yourself and those around you to achieve wholeness and freedom all the time. Every time you read this text, or think about it, your personal power increases. Ever deeper feelings of security and humbleness allow you to let go of all grudges and pettiness. If you like you could start afresh right now, reborn in purity. I have faith in your ability to understand and apply the exercises in this book. Your awareness expands to the area around you. You are wide awake and feeling great!

38

Individual Areas

When you have an understanding of and have experienced the freeing up of your virtues in a general sense you can apply the techniques to individual areas of your life. The wonderful truth is that just as the healing of one virtue helps and uplifts all the other virtues, so the healing of one area of your life produces positive changes in every other area of your life.

Let me give you an example. If you heal an activity such as eating food, you will be creating islands of wellbeing throughout your day. Whenever you eat, you will be reminded consciously or unconsciously of the virtues and any tensions and worries about food will be eliminated giving you greater vitality. Your diet will naturally improve and you will digest food more efficiently supporting your health and improving your clarity of mind. You will be less inclined to overindulge or be swayed by misleading advertising, thus saving you money and you will begin to consume more compassionately. You can choose any activity to heal and uplift such as: getting up in the morning, listening to others, walking and dreaming etc. etc. As well as activities do not overlook other areas such as your appearance, your body, instincts and emotions etc. Further examples are archetypes such as the Protector, the Teacher and the Lover etc. You will see positive changes not only in the chosen area but, to varying degrees, all other areas too.

Here is a technique for healing a particular area of your life:-

39

Exercise Thirteen: Individual Areas

Relax the physical body. Relax inwardly. Silently affirm that you are willing to let go of any false beliefs concerning the area. Love and accept yourself and others doing this activity (or experiencing the area) and the activity or area itself. Let go of any attachments or repulsions that you hold about the activity or area. Choose a virtue (ideally one that you appear to be lacking in the area that you are working on) and allow it to infuse /radiate the concept of the activity or area. Visualise all the virtues as one white light cleansing and uplifting the activity.

40

Independence!

The semi-conscious state is characterised by a false dependency on external conditions. At the moment you may believe that your happiness and peace depend on certain external factors: this is not so. Due to past associations certain qualities within you may only seem able to manifest in certain "favourable" conditions. In actuality these conditions have no power to inhibit or facilitate your positive feelings and virtues, except the power that YOU are pushing onto them. Examples of this inner sickness include: only feeling relaxed when at home, only feeling brave when with friends or only feeling worthy when praised by someone in authority. If you tell yourself that you will be really happy when you win the lottery then you are also telling yourself that you will not (or cannot) be happy until you win the lottery, thus forming a barrier to your happiness now. The next exercise is very effective in weakening and dissolving such false dependencies.

41

Exercise Fourteen: Reclaiming Your Power

Relax inwardly and outwardly. Choose a feeling or quality that seems dependent on an external person or object. Allow yourself to feel whole and blissful right now, embodying the particular feeling/quality: independent of the external person or object. As you breathe in, take back the responsibility and personal power. As you breathe out let go of all past, present and future blaming. Allow yourself to feel whole and complete, joyful and triumphant as you visualise chains breaking. Do this peacefully and joyfully until the false dependency collapses.

42

Summary of Exercise Fourteen: Reclaiming Your Power

In performing this exercise you are associating your breathing process with power, freedom and success. Now whenever you become aware of your breathing, you will get a boost of self-esteem and a feeling of control over your life. If you work at these exercises diligently, you will eventually feel at the optimum healthy state constantly, independent of circumstances.

This exercise will help you to view your past from a higher viewpoint. By asserting your personal responsibility many deep-seated resentments will collapse within you. As you are ultimately responsible for yourself so is everyone else: much deep seated guilt and self-recrimination will collapse within you. You will feel lighter and brighter as many of your complicated strategies to get attention, protect yourself from imagined slights and subconscious self-punishments melt away, revealing a wonderful simplicity that contains all natural and effective strategies in its innocence.

43

The Darkness Within

When you have a good understanding of the virtues and trust their natural power within yourself and others, you will be ready to resolve the darker and more difficult miss comprehensions that you may have been harbouring for a very long time.

In the highest sense, all concepts are equal. It is only our ignorance, coloured by past experience, that makes us prefer or detest one concept over another. There are some concepts that humanity as a whole has shunned and pushed to the darkest and most remote corners of their minds. As you know, when a concept is repressed an area of darkness \ semi-consciousness forms where, over time, many foolish beliefs become lodged. Concepts such as suffering, pain, death, loneliness, abandonment and evil etc., etc. deeply repulse the average person. This powerful repression takes up a lot of energy on a moment to moment basis and the false beliefs can have a crippling effect on our everyday lives. Because they are particularly abhorrent, or at least seem to be, it takes great bravery and compassion to reintegrate them back into our consciousness. That is why I recommend this exercise only to those who already have a good virtuous base of mind. Reintegration of shunned concepts does not mean that we become attracted to them. Reintegration means that we have re-established a state of equilibrium with them: we are neither attracted nor repulsed by them. For example: when confronted with hatred, our minds do not then recoil from it and so fall into semi-conscious habit, we remain present, absolutely conscious, with all our inner qualities available to deal with the situation in the most appropriate way.

44

Exercise Fifteen: Embracing the Darkness

Relax inwardly and outwardly. Visualise the unified white light of all the virtues vibrating through every part of you, cleansing, protecting healing and energising you: actually radiating out beyond your physical body, uplifting the atmosphere around you. Choose a concept that is normally shunned such as death, decay or suffering etc. Let go of any false beliefs you may be holding about it. Endeavour to attune to that part of your being which already loves and accepts all concepts equally. Allow your consciousness to penetrate and mingle with the highest and most healthy appreciation of the concept you have chosen to reintegrate. Silently declare that you are willing for your inner and outer life to transform: willing to let go of any misguided notions and habits connected with the concept. Actually see, in your mind's eye, the darkness falling away from you as your feelings of bliss and compassion increase.

Summary of Exercise Fifteen: Embracing the Darkness

If you perform this exercise correctly, you will appreciate that, by shunning concepts in the past, you have been rejecting many qualities within yourself and have viewed reality through a distorted and negative lens. Here are some examples illustrating the importance of integrating the generally shunned concepts back into your consciousness:

Death and decay are natural processes within you. When you withdraw your attention energy from a belief or habit it begins to decay and die. The cells of your body are constantly dying and being replaced by healthy and vigorous new cells. In both these cases and others, the beneficial processes of decay and death can be inhibited and disrupted if the consciousness shuns the corresponding concepts. Furthermore death and decay are inescapable facts of life. By deeply accepting this we will not fall into the trap of becoming too attached to things that by their very nature are transient and fleeting. Such attachment is the cause of suffering.

If we fear failure and shun the concept within us we will tend to not even try and so achieve nothing anyway - wasting opportunities. Or we will strive so hard that all the fun is taken out of our striving, we fall into ruthlessness and then become devastated if our goal eludes us after all. Furthermore every failure contains within it the keys and subtle clues for future success. Thus if we let our minds recoil away from our past failures then we are denying ourselves proper access to the valuable data which they contain.

If we fear rejection and abandonment, we may find ourselves acting against our better judgement merely to pander to those who do not have our best interests at heart. We may feel constrained to the mainstream and feel unable to resist unhealthy traditions or practices because of our deep felt need to feel accepted.

Each of the negative aspects in these examples can be easily resolved by reintegrating the corresponding concepts and applying the other techniques in this book. Can you think of any other examples of benefits arising from reintegrating shunned concepts? If you cannot and you are serious about liberating your vast potential, then you should try hard to come up with some examples of your own: independent and creative thought, along with a healthy curiosity, are all essential characteristics of a successful inner worker.

46

Improving Your Practice

The material in this section is indirectly covered in the previous sections but, because of its importance, I have reserved this final section for its study. This section is the last, but you should also see it as the beginning of your REAL study, for that is what it is. When you have studied this chapter carefully and applied yourself to EXERCISE SIXTEEN you should rest for a few days so that your mind can assimilate the changes. Then go back to the start of the book and reread it with fresh eyes, freer from the limitations and prejudices that you carried with you the first time round. You will find a real sense of purpose in your life as every day you achieve greater depths of wholeness and personal security.

To improve your practice you should first become aware of any problems that you have concerning it and then direct your efforts accordingly. For example, if you are afraid to change, you should work on your bravery. If you are disinterested, you should work on your curiosity and if you feel incapable, you should work on your majesty. By doing this, you are actually turning the problem into a stepping stone to success.

At the moment you may see this book as mere entertainment- a distraction from your everyday problems. You may feel that the exercises will only have a slight beneficial effect on you or be holding other limiting ideas about your practice. This book is in tune with that part of your nature that wants the best for you. It is a comprehensive reminder of things that, deep down, you have always known. As you reread this book keep in mind that profound changes for the better are not only possible: they are inevitable as long as you apply yourself to the exercises. To achieve profound inner cleansing and transformation, a great desire and determination are needed as well as skilful means. This book provides the skilful means but you must provide the desire and determination yourself.

Exercise Sixteen: Boosting Practice

Relax physically and inwardly. Allow yourself to feel a real sense of personal freedom, realising that nothing is set in stone and that you have the power to shape your life and control your destiny. Inwardly acknowledge that you are responsible for your experience. Simply let go of all ideas to do with blaming others for your misfortunes. As you breathe in, visualise the personal power that you had previously pushed onto others flowing back into you. As you breathe out, visualise your compassion as light radiating from every part of you, healing and uplifting those in need. Breathe peacefully and easily when doing this exercise without strain or undue effort. Remember to maintain a state of inner and outer relaxation during this exercise. Allow yourself to smile gently as you simply breathe in and out, building up a feeling of well-being and real personal power.

By gently relaxing even more, allow a profound and loving sense of concern for the wellbeing of every part of yourself to support and heighten the good work that you have accomplished.

Focus your attention on the concept of your inner Healer and your inner Liberator. Become aware of their power flowing through you, changing your awareness.

Now allow yourself to embody the concepts of the perfect student and the perfect patient. Let your concepts of being a student and being a patient become one with the white light of the virtues. Visualise the wonderful light transforming and uplifting you in many beneficial ways, making you ready to study effectively in accordance with your highest good.

Final Word

You may appreciate that this knowledge has profound implications not just for the individual but also for society as a whole. It can remedy just as surely the ills of society on a global scale as it has on the personal scale. It is an antidote to the lopsided views of today's citizen but, perhaps more importantly, it also has a role in inoculating future generations from countless unbalanced views which they may otherwise fall prey to. When this type of information begins, slowly but surely, to inform the policy makers of this world we will see many so called inevitable social problems dissolve away.

If you have any questions or comments please feel free to write to me at VirtueScience.com and I will do my best to answer you. I believe that this virtue-based inner medicine is an evolving science of great benefit to Humanity. I welcome any insights or contributions you personally have to offer.

Made in the USA
Charleston, SC
29 January 2015